Edwin Sánchez:
The Short Plays

D1412487

BROADWAY PLAY PUBLISHING INC
224 E 62nd St, NY, NY 10065
www.broadwayplaypub.com
info@broadwayplaypub.com

Cover art by Daniel Jay Rubin

First printing: June 2016
I S B N: 978-0-88145-639-4

Book design: Marie Donovan
Page make-up: Adobe InDesign
Typeface: Palatino
Printed and bound in the U S A

CONTENTS

BEA AND MAY

CHARACTERS & SETTING

BEA
MAY

The dressing area of a chapel

(BEA *enters. She looks at* MAY, *dressed as a bride.* BEA *is 50,* MAY *is 30. Ish. Emphasis on the ish.*)

BEA: May.

MAY: Bea.

(BEA *and* MAY *kiss. The kiss suddenly grows in passion until* MAY *breaks it off. They separate and stare at each other.*)

BEA: It wasn't so much what I could have, it was all about what I couldn't have. That is what keeps me up at night. Looking at you, knowing you don't care. Knowing you'd just as soon set me on fire as look at me, well, baby, that's just candy. That's just chocolate.

MAY: You missed the bridal shower.

BEA: Did I? I'll catch the next one.

MAY: There's not going to be a next one.

BEA: Uh huh. Let's go with that for now. So.

MAY: So.

BEA: We doing it?

(*Silence*)

Okay. We're not. But we'll still see each other?

MAY: In passing.

BEA: That's always been the best way with you.

MAY: You said you'd play nice.

BEA: You want me to play nice?

(MAY *checks herself in the mirror.*)

MAY: I knew I shouldn't have hired you as the caterer.

BEA: You needed at least one person you loved at your wedding.

MAY: You know, my mother once told me—

BEA: Oh God—

MAY: She told me that with age comes wisdom.

BEA: What was she, a hundred and five?

MAY: No. But she said the best thing, and you have to realize that I never listened to my mother, I mean, I'd rather chew glass than listen to her.

BEA: I would glaze over when my mother talked to me.

MAY: Color me surprised. Anyway, my mother said the best thing, she said, later in life, someone will ask you, "who was the great love of your life?" and you'll be able to answer. Without remorse. Just a sort of "oh yeah, that was them". So and so was the love of my life. And somehow, you missed it.

BEA: And that would be me.

MAY: No, that would be the man I'm about to marry. But, you would be in the top ten.

BEA: Do you have anything to drink?

MAY: How's that?

BEA: Alcohol. A drink. A cocktail.

MAY: No. It's a dry wedding. Good Lord, woman, you're the caterer, you must know we're driving this thing dry.

BEA: Vicks Formula 44? In a flask. On your thigh.

(*Pause.* MAY *retrieves a flask from under her dress.*)

MAY: Ice?

BEA: Straight up.

MAY: I can do that.

BEA: He doesn't know you drink, does he? God knows you're of age.

MAY: So sayeth the A A R P card holder.

BEA: Ouch. That's gonna leave a mark. And so uncalled for.

MAY: I calls em like I sees em.

BEA: And how do you see me?

MAY: Lonely.

BEA: Can't be sued for libel on that one.

MAY: I've seen you in love, in heartbreak, in total despair.

BEA: Yeah, well.

MAY: You know why, don't you?

BEA: Sweet Lord, she's going to tell me.

MAY: Because you're obsessed with me. You're obsessed with me because I'm unattainable.

BEA: Egomaniac, your table is ready.

MAY: You've watched me fall in love, you've seen me marry a man.

BEA: Or two.

MAY: George didn't count.

BEA: Why, cause you caught him in your wedding dress?

MAY: Well, yeah. That should count as a deal breaker.

BEA: And who did you run to when it was all over?

MAY: To you. Where else would I run? Don't you know that some people are not meant to last a lifetime?

BEA: So, the new man in your life?

MAY: Jerry. Very sweet. Very rich.

BEA: And you love him?

MAY: I love the fact that he's grateful. And generous. That he makes no demands.

BEA: So, who does he look like?

MAY: The truth? Rosie O'Donnell.

(BEA *laughs*.)

MAY: He looks like an old woman. You know how some men look genderless when they get to a certain age? That's Jerry.

BEA: And he's rich?

MAY: Comfortable. *(Pause)* Okay, rich. Filthy rich. Disgustingly rich.

BEA: Money trumps love.

(MAY *shrugs*.)

MAY: Tell me what money doesn't trump. I'll wait.

BEA: Your son is going to give you away? He doesn't know about us, does he?

MAY: If you ever tell him—

BEA: I won't.

MAY: I would never talk to you again.

BEA: I wish you well.

MAY: Yeah, right.

BEA: No, I do.

(The Wedding March *starts*.)

BEA: Ah, they're playing your song. It belongs to you. To a man and a woman.

MAY: Bea—

BEA: I swore I'd play nice.

MAY: I'm not going to fight with you.

BEA: I'm tired of fighting. For all the good times we've had, there have been too many battle scars. Everytime we've kissed I felt as if my head were being held underwater. As if I were dying from a lack of oxygen.

MAY: Get the door.

BEA: Thirty seconds. A bride's supposed to make an entrance. I'm dying.

(MAY *stops.*)

BEA: Bouquet up. ...I will be dead in under a year. It's irreversible.

MAY: What? Don't do this to me.

BEA: And oddly enough it's still about you. I swear, it's a gift. I'm releasing you, May. Letting you go. But I had to tell you.

MAY: To ruin my day.

BEA: To make sure when you heard about it, it would be from me, so you wouldn't feel guilty. That's not the right word. You wouldn't feel...guilty, I don't know if you'd feel anything. God forbid you should feel something. They're starting the wedding march again. They can start it up to three times before they send someone back here. Three times is cute. It's "isn't the bride nervous" as opposed to, "did she open a window and make a break for it?"

MAY: Why didn't you tell me anything?

BEA: I'm telling you now. I hear some nervous twitters out there. I'm getting married myself. Tomorrow.

MAY: Don't joke.

BEA: Lovely girl. Woman. Older than the hills. Unattractive. Humorless. And loves me without measure. Has already promised to be there during the worst of it.

MAY: *(Looking at the door)* Tell me you're lying. Tell me you're not dying.

BEA: And she'll do all this knowing she's my second choice.

(MAY embraces BEA.)

BEA: Don't make me slap you on your wedding day. The music stopped.

MAY: Oh crap, Jerry's coming up the aisle.

BEA: Tell him it's bad luck to see the bride before the wedding.

MAY: *(Calling out through a crack in the door)* Don't you dare come in here. Zipper problem. I'll be right out.

BEA: And he believed you.

MAY: I'll cancel the honeymoon. I'll just stay in town, and take care of you.

BEA: No, that's Shelia's job. That's her name. She would do anything for me.

MAY: But you don't love her.

BEA: A minor detail. They're playing your song again. A little more tentatively this time. Those little pauses between the dum-dum-dah-dum.

(MAY gets to the door, stops.)

MAY: Jerry's rich. I can take care of you. I marry him, and I promise to take care of you. The best of everything. I swear. *(Silence)* Don't be stupid. You won't want for anything. Everything you need. Please. Let me do this for you.

BEA: And if I told you the one thing I needed, the one thing I wanted, was for you to walk out of here. With me. Could you do that?

(MAY *hesitates, takes* BEA*'s hand. Goes towards the door that* BEA *came in through at the beginning.* BEA *stops her.*)

BEA: No. Through the other door. Through the door where all your family is waiting for you to come through. Take my hand and walk me through that door.

(MAY *stops. She begins to cry. She can't do it.* BEA *covers* MAY*'s face with her veil.*)

BEA: Go. Get married. I was lying.

MAY: No, you weren't.

BEA: No. I wasn't. But, if you don't have the strength to love me, how would you have the strength to help me die? This is going to be the last image I see of you. Be a pretty bride for Bea.

(MAY *takes a flower from her bouquet, gives it to* BEA. MAY *exits.* BEA *holds the flower, kisses it.*)

BEA: That's. Gonna leave a mark. (*She exits.*)

END OF PLAY

CELESTED

CHARACTERS & SETTING

Celeste
Lou

Outside of a hotel ballroom

(The outside of a hotel ballroom. Typical wedding celebration music is heard. CELESTE *is outside the door, her phone in her hand. An angry* LOU *enters, his cell phone in hand.)*

LOU: I cannot believe you!

CELESTE: She in there?

LOU: She's the bride! Of course she's in there.

CELESTE: She pretty? I could only see the back of her head at the church?

*(*LOU *glares at* CELESTE.*)*

CELESTE: Damn it to hell, she's gorgeous, huh. Well brides are always beautiful, that glow you know.

LOU: You need to leave.

CELESTE: Or is it first time mothers? Well, she's both, so it's a win win for her.

LOU: I got the first dance, I gotta go. And so do you.

CELESTE: I texted you.

LOU: During the ceremony!

CELESTE: And you looked. I can't believe you looked. Must have pissed her off.

LOU: *(As in intro)* Celeste, Timing, Timing, Celeste.

CELESTE: How many times did we break up? *(She sucks her teeth to indicate a huge number.)*

LOU: And how many times did I come crawling back?

CELESTE: All but this last time. So far.

LOU: I should…

CELESTE: So far.

LOU: I'm going back in.

CELESTE: You know what I would do if I were you?

LOU: Goodbye, Celeste.

CELESTE: I would dance my last dance with me, before you dance your first dance with her.

LOU: Don't do this.

CELESTE: Why not? You scared? *(She kisses* LOU.*)* Why would you be scared?

LOU: Cause if I do. *(He kisses her.)* I'll remember every evil thing you ever did to me.

CELESTE: You love her?

LOU: I love her even more than I hate you. I could never hate anybody as much as I hate you.

CELESTE: Wow. There was a moment

LOU: a moment, when I saw

CELESTE: you

LOU: you, just now, a second

CELESTE: a moment, that I

LOU: that I

CELESTE: The music stopped.

LOU: That's my cue. *(He exits.)*

END OF PLAY

DING!

CHARACTERS & SETTING

1
2
3
4

A waiting room

(Three people sit in a waiting room.)

(DING!)

2: *(To 1 who is lost in thought)* I think that's you.

(No reaction from 1)

2: Excuse me?

3: *(To 1)* Hey hon, you're up.

1: You go ahead.

3: It's not my turn.

2: We just can't jump out of line.

1: Sure we can, it's no problem. Go ahead. Or you. Either one, doesn't matter.

(DING!)

2: *(To ding)* He's on his way!

1: No, I'm not.

(4 enters.)

4: Chop chop, what's the hold up? Six hours of labor, I think she's ready.

1: I'm not.

4: What?

1: I don't want to get born again.

2: Wait, are we allowed to do that?

3: Ssssh.

4: You're being reborn, your soul is entering the baby. It's a wonderful thing.

3: I can't wait for it to be my turn.

4: See?

1: I don't want to do it. I don't want go back. Last time wasn't that great.

3: Great for me, I won an Oscar.

4: See? You gotta dream big.

(DING!)

1: You say dream big, great. And when those dreams don't come true, huh? When you just become old and angry and bitter?

3: That's up to each of us.

4: Exactly.

1: It isn't though. We leave here full of hope and then Slam!

(DING!)

2: We're having a problem here.

4: There is no problem. You have to go back. There are things you didn't do, things you have to make up for.

1: I want a guarantee.

3: Wait, that's just ridiculous.

1: *(To 3)* Do you control the ding? No. Then shut up.

4: What do you want?

1: I...I want whatever makes me special not to be beaten out of me by life, I want dreams that don't have a shelf life, I want some big tangible wins.

4: There are no guarantees. Ever.

1: Then why should I go back?

4: Cause you'll never stop saying "what if?" if you don't.

(1 *goes to door.*)

(*DING!*)

1: I can't. All I remember is a lifetime of small failures. Not even big ones, not glamorous ones, just small.

4: You won't remember them. You're going to be a very hopeful kid.

1: ...Let's do this.

(*DING!*)

(1 *closes his eyes tight. Opens them. He is born.*)

END OF PLAY

ERNESTO THE MAGNIFICENT

CHARACTER & SETTING

Ernesto

A stage

(A man in a tuxedo which has obviously seen better days, takes center stage. He walks with a very stiff leg.)

ERNESTO: Hello, my name is Ernesto the Magnificent! I said, "my name is Ernesto the Magnificent." Hold for applause. I'll wait. I have performed for presidents, crowned heads of state and film stars from around the world. And yet, somehow tonight, I am here with you. What a thrill. Prepare to be amazed, for I am, drum roll please.

(There is no drum roll. He sighs.)

A FIRE EATER!!!!! Now you are impressed, no? My remarkable feats of derring-do have astounded and confounded young and old alike. Fire is primal, fire is sexy, fire, she is, dangerous. The heat. Enveloping you, swallowing you, until you—disappear. Having said that, however, my agent in his infinite wisdom has seen fit to book me in a club where even a match cannot be lit onstage without an overzealous Fire Marshall wrestling you to the ground so that he can beat you unconscious with a fire extinguisher. Charming, no? But not to worry, for tonight Ernesto the Magnificent becomes Ernesto the Stupendous going where no man has gone before. Behold!

(He pulls a sword out of his pant let. After a moment he winces.)

I'm okay. Yes tonight, for your viewing pleasure, Ernesto will swallow this sword! Feel free to gasp. Go ahead.

(He hisses.)

Gasp!

(After a beat, satisfied)

This is a real sword. Not some dummied up prop where the blade disappears into the handle. Yesssss, even Ernesto is amazed. I have, once again, amazed myself.

(He takes the sword, leans his head back and positions the sword over his open mouth. Beat. He lowers the sword.)

I should point out that Ernesto the Fearless has never actually done this act. But I have been cheating death my entire life, so I am not afraid.

(He again lifts the sword, tilts his head back and opens his mouth. Again he lowers the sword.)

For what is there to fear, but fear itself. A very great man once said that. Yes, he did.

A very, very great man.

(He looks at the sword, runs his finger along the blade.)

A sharp, great man.

(He raises the sword, but stops midway, brings it down. He loses his accent.)

My father was the one who did the fire eater act, and his father before him and so on and so forth. This is my legacy. No matter if I wanted it or not. Imagine being born and being given a book of matches and being told, that's it kid, that's your lot in life. Maybe I didn't like fire or maybe I wanted to be an arsonist, not as a career you know, but more like a hobby. But no, no choice for Ernesto. I hate that name! First time I did the act I was eight years old. The novelty of having a child fire eater, what won't they think of next? It was a beauty pageant. First my grandfather came out, then my father. I was saved for last. On stage with

fifty of the most beautiful girls from the United States.
I brought the flame up to my lips, sweat pouring off
me, hand shaking, and at the worst possible moment
I get a sneezing attack. I didn't swallow the fire, I spit
it out and all of sudden all these girls with their over
sprayed, moussed and geled hair are going up like
roman candles. It was like Dante's Inferno, if Dante's
inferno had an evening gown competition. Red and
Blue states running amok, crashing into each other,
while I continued, unable to control my sneezing. Until
like an asthmatic dragon, only faint sparks remained to
punctuate my fiery debacle. My father and grandfather
were finally able to get close enough to me and began
beating me right on stage. "It's fire eating, NOT fire
breathing! You've ruined us! Ruined us!" And all
I'm thinking is I'm sorry, I'm sorry, I'm sorry. ...But
tonight Ernesto the Failure gets to carve out a new
identity for himself. One where he is not the source of
disappointment to a fire breathing father but rather
a rebel, capable of a greatness his father could only
dream of, could only hope to attain. Could only aspire
to if he were half the fucking man I am! Who stands
here with a mother fucking sword while he and every
other lame-o man in my family coat their lips with
enough flame retardant for an Alaskan oil spill, but
hey, somehow I'm the loser, I'm the wannabe, I'm the
nothing!!!!

(Pause. He resumes his accent.)

Please forgive Ernesto. Sometimes I am reminded of
why I envy orphans. So please, welcome, Ernesto, His
Own Man.

(He lifts the sword, tilts his head back, the sword poised over
his mouth. He turns to face the audience while holding the
pose.)

Remember, whatever doesn't kill us only makes us stronger. Or is that, whatever doesn't kill us leaves us scarred for life? No matter.

(He again faces the point of the sword.)

Okay, dad, top this.

(He slowly begins to lower the sword towards his open mouth. Blackout)

END OF PLAY

ETHAN'S GOT GAME

CHARACTER & SETTING

ETHAN

A grassy area by a lake

(ETHAN, *a teenage boy, wet and drying his hair, sits by a lake. He takes a swig from a beer bottle. Next to him is a pail of golf balls. He calls out to his friend who is still in the lake.*)

ETHAN: No, Willis, the other side.

(*He points.*)

I already looked where you are. Now we're looking for a golf ball with a blue stripe around it. That's Mister Allen's favorite. He'll pay extra for that one. "Sentimental value".

(*Snorts*)

Old fool.

(*Drinks again and holds up the pail*)

Hey look, Willis, I got the town by the balls! Guess when you're old your balls mean a lot to you. Hell, they're old enough. Youngest golfer here is forty if he's a day. They got so much free time, spend their days swinging a club at a little ball. Already made their money, they're set. Not me. But I'm gonna be a millionaire before I'm twenty one, you watch. Okay, so this is small fry stuff, chump change, but it's a start. This and the other three businesses I got going is gonna take me up and out. You find Mr. Allen's ball tonight and I'll think about taking you with me.

(*Waves to Willis and watches him disappear under water.*)

No I won't. Won't take anybody. Just be rich and alone. Finally.

(*Picks up one of the balls from the pail.*)

Now, how is something like this supposed to have
sentimental value? A person, a person who leaves,
now that has sentimental value. I mean, I can't go into
a sporting goods store and buy a new father, right?
Or buy back my mother's life so she's not tired all the
time. Or get Ainsley one of her own so she ain't always
trying to share mine. She's just like mama, a born loser.

(To Willis)

You find anything? Well haul yourself outta there. I got
V C Rs to fix.
Gotta be successful. Papa left cause he couldn't do it. I
can. I will.

(Studies one of the balls)

I got a blue magic marker at home. Make you real
pretty. Yep, looks like I found your ball, Mister Allen.

END OF PLAY

GOODBYE

CHARACTERS & SETTING

HIJO
PAPI
MAMI
HERMANA
ABUELA
YOUNGER HIJO

The doorway of a small home

(*A young man,* HIJO, *hurries onstage, carrying a folding chair. He sits. This is the first of four chairs that will make up a car.*)

HIJO: C'mon, papi! I don't want to miss my plane.

(PAPI *enters, with his chair and sits as if he's in the driver's seat.*)

PAPI: New York's not gonna go anyplace. It'll wait for you.

HIJO: Next time you see me I'll be a working actor, I promise. And I'll never play a pimp, a drug dealer or a gang member, I swear to you. C'mon, let's go!!

(MAMI *comes out with her chair, sits behind* PAPI. *She has a paper bag.*)

MAMI: *Mira* hijito, here are some sandwiches. They never feed you on planes anymore.

HIJO: Ma!

(HERMANA *runs out with her chair, sits behind* HIJO.)

HERMANA: I'm keeping anything you left behind!

(HERMANA *hits* HIJO, *who hits her back.* ABUELA *enters, wedges herself between* MAMI *and* HERMANA.)

ABUELA: *Dejenme un ladito.* (*She takes out a rosary and begins to pray.*)

HIJO: Why is she praying, I haven't died!

(MAMI *slaps the back of* HIJO's *head.*)

MAMI: *Respeta!*

(YOUNGER HIJO *comes running in and sits on* HIJO's *lap.*)

YOUNGER HIJO: I want to bring the dog!

HIJO: No way!

(*Three* COUSINS *come running in.*)

COUSINS: Cousin, wait for us!!!

(*Somehow the three* COUSINS *wedge themselves into the car. There are now nine people in the car.*)

HIJO: This is ridiculous!!!!

PAPI: No, this is your family. We're part of your dreams, wherever you go.

(The rest of the actors come and stand around the car, looking straight out, with big hopeful smiles. HIJO looks around the crammed car full of his family and his anger fades. He smiles and calls out to a dog off stage.

HIJO: *(Whistles)* Hey Tongo, here boy! We're going to the airport!

END OF PLAY

JIMMY

CHARACTERS & SETTING

DANNY
JIMMY

A small, undistinguished living room

DANNY: Come in. Close the door. Let's have a look at you.

(JIMMY *enters, turns.*)

DANNY: Slowly.

(JIMMY *turns slowly.*)

DANNY: Very nice. Would you like me to do the same?

(JIMMY *shrugs.*)

You're right. Let's save something for later. Thank you for actually wearing pants that fit you. I detest those pants that just hang off guys nowadays, don't you?

JIMMY: Mmm hmm.

DANNY: Certainly they provide easy access, but so little else.

JIMMY: I don't take it up the ass.

DANNY: Sssh. Please. So you said.

JIMMY: So you here on business?

DANNY: Small talk. Wonderful.

JIMMY: I thought you might need time to warm up or something. Let the viagra kick in.

DANNY: Perhaps I should have spent a little more and gotten someone with a personality.

JIMMY: Come on, you're not so old. (*He puts his hand on* DANNY's *crotch.*) You know what to do.

(DANNY *takes* JIMMY's *hand off his crotch.*)

DANNY: Yes, I do. And it's my party so we're going to take it a little slower.

JIMMY: Let me see the money.

DANNY: You're wise to the ways of the world. I like that. So am I. *(Shows* JIMMY *a hundred dollar bill, puts it away.)* This is half of it. You will get the rest of your fee upon a satisfactory completion of your task.

JIMMY: What if you stiff me?

DANNY: Oh, I'm hoping to. What's this? A smile?

JIMMY: Look, no offense

DANNY: Why do people say that just before they offend you?

JIMMY: Why are we here? This is an S R O, this is a terrible place. How can you afford two hundred dollars for me, plus a tip.

DANNY: You know, I like that you're curious. It's the sign of an open mind. It's a simple story really, boy meets boy, boy loves boy, boy loses boy and every year on the anniversary of their declaration of love, reenacts it. There, now isn't that a charming little tale, Mark?

JIMMY: Jimmy.

DANNY: You're on the clock now, you're Mark.

*(*JIMMY *shrugs.)*

DANNY: Mark was incredibly wealthy, when you're incredibly wealthy you don't say rich, you say wealthy, and he just fell madly in love with me at first sight. But to see if I could love him just for himself he pretended to live in this very room, so I naturally assumed he had nothing. Then came the night when he was sure of my love and he pulled out all the stops, everything that night was the best of the best as he vowed his everlasting love for me.

JIMMY: Okay, got it. We're recreating that night.

DANNY: Bright. You're just so bright.

JIMMY: Is Mark dead?

DANNY: There's a flower by the door. A single rose. I want you to present it to me.

(JIMMY *gets the rose.*)

JIMMY: Here.

(Pause. DANNY *motions "and?")*

JIMMY: ...Uh, this is for you.

DANNY: Mark, how incredibly kind and thoughtful of you. I'm sure you could barely afford this.

JIMMY: ...Yeah, well, you know.

DANNY: Take my hand, look into my eyes and tell me how beautiful I am.

JIMMY: You're beautiful.

DANNY: You really think so?

JIMMY: Am I answering as me or Mark?

DANNY: Pour us some champagne. The bottles already opened.

(JIMMY *does.*)

DANNY: Now make a toast.

(JIMMY *just stares at* DANNY, *lost.*)

DANNY: I've written one out for you on the napkin.

JIMMY: *(Reads)* "To Danny, the most beautiful boy in the world." *(To* DANNY, *as himself.)* How old is this napkin?

DANNY: And you want a tip?

JIMMY: *(Reads)* "Stay with me forever. Make me the happiest man in the world."

DANNY: Now we clink glasses, sip. And kiss me gently on the mouth. Or don't you kiss?

JIMMY: No, I like kissing.

(DANNY *and* JIMMY *kiss.*)

JIMMY: Then what happened?

DANNY: Oh, Mark confessed everything, and we made love.

JIMMY: Finally.

DANNY: And I moved into the land of plenty.

JIMMY: He must have had it bad for you.

DANNY: He was crazy for me.

JIMMY: And you keep this little room for…?

DANNY: Sentimental reasons. Actually, I own the entire building.

JIMMY: Uh huh.

DANNY: Usually I live on my yacht, going where the mood takes me.

JIMMY: Because you're so rich.

DANNY: Paté? It's the finest money can buy.

JIMMY: It's cat food.

DANNY: I beg your pardon.

JIMMY: That's cat food. I saw the empty can by the door when I went back to get the rose. I wanted to see how far you'd go with this. Give me the hundred and I won't beat the crap out of you.

(DANNY *gives him the hundred.* JIMMY *looks at it.*)

JIMMY: It's not real.

DANNY: Nothing is.

JIMMY: No, my anger is real.

DANNY: Before you do anything that only one of us is going to regret, hear me out, if nothing else I've taught you a valuable lesson. There's going to come a time for you too when you're going to be standing on the pier as you watch your youth sail off without you. Gone. Never to return. And the most you can hope for is that what remains is a benevolent caricature of the you that you once were.

JIMMY: So all this was so I would call you beautiful?

DANNY: You did.

JIMMY: But I didn't mean it.

DANNY: And the kiss?

JIMMY: I especially didn't mean the kiss. *(Silence)* So no Mark?

DANNY: There were many Marks. Until I ran out of them.

JIMMY: What happened to all the money you got? The gifts?

DANNY: I spent it. Gave it away. So you see, I've actually done you a favor. I've given you a glimpse of what your future is going to be.

(JIMMY punches DANNY sending him sprawling on the couch.)

JIMMY: Okay, first up, take a look at this.

(JIMMY throws DANNY a bank book.)

DANNY: What the?

JIMMY: That my man, is a bank book, where my balance is twenty thousand dollars. In another year, I'm going to double it.

DANNY: How good do you think you are at what you do?

JIMMY: Between photo shoots, private parties and my web site I'll make enough in five years to pay for law school. Yeah, I'm going to be a lawyer, get the joke out of the way now.

DANNY: I got nothing.

JIMMY: When I graduate I'll have made enough contacts to intern in one of the top law firms in the country where I will work my way up to partner by the time I'm thirty five.

DANNY: And of course this will all happen just as you said.

JIMMY: Give me one reason why it shouldn't. Not opinion, reason. You? You like to live in the past because that's where your promise lived. Me? I can't wait for tomorrow. I can't wait to be fifty and sixty and seventy, with a duplex apartment and a house in the country. I usually don't do this but here. *(He takes out a hundred dollar bill from a wad of money.)* You made me laugh. Go sit in a dark bar, you might have another Mark in your future. Just make sure it's a really dark bar. *(He is about to leave.)*

DANNY: If things don't work out the way you planned, I'll save a bar stool for you. And I'll be kind. I'll even call you beautiful.

(JIMMY returns, about to kick DANNY who is still on the ground, but he stops himself.)

JIMMY: I won't be you. I'd kill myself first.

DANNY: Where have I heard that before? Oh that's right, I said it. Many years ago.

(JIMMY exits.)

END OF PLAY

JODY'S MOTHER

CHARACTER & SETTING

JODY'S MOTHER

A confessional

(*At rise:* JODY'S MOTHER *kneels in a confessional. She crosses herself.*)

JODY'S MOTHER: Forgive me Father for I have sinned. It has been a week since my last confession. A week. Or a lifetime. Take your pick. …It's so quiet in here. Finally. I just want to enjoy the silence for a moment. Sanctuary! I'm sorry, they had "Hunchback of Notre Dame" on last week. I love that movie. Maureen O'Hara, gorgeous, Charles Laughton, less so, he's the freak. He dies at the end. He has too. I don't watch T V much anymore. They sneak stuff in on you. You're watching some "Full House" rerun and the local newscaster cuts in with "Mother of accused pedophile goes out for milk and cigarettes, more at eleven." And I sit there knowing they're talking about me. Jody came to us, last week, his father and me are in the middle of "Jeopardy" and suddenly Jody is standing there. Looking down at the floor, shifting from one foot to the other. His father tells him to tie his shoelaces, he looks like a punk. Jody's forty one but he dresses like a teenager. It never bothered me cause the younger he looked the younger I could tell people I was, right? Jody ignores his father, which he does all the time, and I'm thinking, "Oh, no, not another fight." And then Jody says, "I'm gonna be on Dateline tonight. Don't say anything. In ten minutes. Don't say anything. They made it look like I was doing something bad, but I wasn't. I swear. I was just, visiting a friend, that's all. Please, don't say anything." And we didn't. We just sat there as the show started and the host told us about a

sting operation to trap pedophiles. On line predators.
Jody spends all his time on his computer. He tells me
he's working. He lives at home, he doesn't have a
job, but he's working. Dateline shows all these men
arriving at this house, about two hours from where
we live, and they all think they're going to have sex
with a little boy, but then the camera crew pops out
and it's all over. Their lives are over and we feel no
sympathy for them whatsoever. They're evil. They're
getting what they deserve. Still, no Jody. And then
the announcer say, "And when we come back, the
worst predator of the lot. You won't believe what our
cameras caught." And we hardly breathe for the next
few minutes, while people on T V joke about beer and
a baby sings, "I'm a big kid now." Jody is still standing,
looking expectantly at the screen. We all are. The show
is back and somebody from the sting operation has
decided to make it more interesting. The next man
has been asked by the little boy to come in through
the garage and bring a six pack of beer with him. "Oh,
and take off all your clothes. I'll be naked, too. Happy
face." And then we see Jody. He doesn't know that an
outside camera is filming him as he circles the house.
I hear my husband as he pleads under his breath,
"Don't go in." Just like you do to the hero when you're
watching a horror movie. But Jody goes in. And at
that moment our life is over. Of course he takes off his
clothes in the garage. Of course the reporter and the
news crew catch him on tape when he enters the house
looking for the little boy. Jody looks numb. He sits
there wrapped in a towel someone threw at him. He
calls the reporter, "sir". He swears he's never done this
before. My husband is dry sobbing now. Tears coming
from so deep inside him that his chest makes a sickly
hollow sound. Me? I'm watching. I have to see every
last detail. The reporter finally lets Jody go, who gets
to the garage door and doesn't know if he's supposed

to give the towel back. Someone on the camera crew snickers. But there's more. Jody's the star of this show. The reporter tells us that Jody has apparently gone home and gone right back on line. He's made a date for the very next day. And there is Jody, in broad daylight, outside of McDonald's, waiting for another little boy. I couldn't hear the rest of the show. There were people outside our window, screaming, cursing. Jody's father takes off his belt and begins to beat Jody, like he used to do when he was a little boy, and Jody rolls up in a ball on the floor and lets his father beat him. On T V Jody tries to outrun the camera crew who focus on his untied sneaker laces. Comedy relief. We finally go to bed, don't know when. None of us sleep. The name calling dies down, but it's Friday, so people get drunk and it starts up again every so often. I want to call the police but my husband says "no", and the way he said it, this frightened little voice, made me put the phone down. I get up. Stand outside Jody's door and see the light from under the door. I hear his fingers on the keyboard. He's on line. I put my hand on the doorknob and try to open the door as quietly as possible, but it's locked. "Jody", I call out, in a voice I don't recognize. And in an equally unfamiliar voice he answers, "I'm working, ma." I make my husband leave town, "Just for a couple of weeks", I tell him. I love this man. I have loved him for over forty years. I will always love him. I stay home. With Jody. I run the errands. People point, spit, stare. I don't say anything. At night I look at baby pictures of Jody, his school pictures, family pictures. I'm looking for the moment when he stopped being my Jody. I realize he hasn't. He's still my boy. The one who never forgets my birthday and listens to me tell the same story over and over. This sweater? He gave me this sweater. I didn't care that he still lived at home, that he couldn't hold a job. Some people take longer to find themselves than other people. And then sometimes, they find themselves when you're not looking and there's nothing you can do to change them. I am so deathly afraid that if I ask him what he wants to do with these boys, he'll tell me. He's rationalized it. When he was fifteen I caught him with a seven year old boy. He told me they were playing. The little boy's eyes were nervous, all over the place and Jody, my Jody, was out of breath. But he looked so happy. I told them to come downstairs, we're going to sing Happy Birthday now. And I closed the door and later served them cake and I never looked back. I hadn't seen anything. Just two boys playing. Before he went to bed Jody kissed me goodnight and told me he loved me. I told him I loved him, too. I still do. I left the house at eight am this morning. Jody had his breakfast and took his lunch into his room. He'll only leave his room now for dinner. I thought of breaking his computer, selling it, but he'd just get another one. Even if it meant selling his own blood, he would just get another one. Before I left, I turned on the gas and left the oven door open. He won't feel a thing. He'll just sleep. Like a baby. And I'll go home and join him. I'll hold his hand and sing to him. Pain can't follow you, obsession can't follow you. It has to stay behind. If you can't take the good stuff with you when you go, then you can't take the bad stuff either. It stays back, with everything that's weighed us down and all we take with us is light, even if we've lived in darkness. We are suddenly surrounded by light. And forgiveness.

END OF PLAY

LILI MARLENE

CHARACTER & SETTING

Lili Marlene, *a beauteous woman of an indeterminate age, enters. She wears a glamorous evening gown and faces the audience.*

A stage

LILI MARLENE: Hello ladies and gentlemen. It is my great privilege to be with you tonight. Don't let the accent fool you. I am one hundred percent Yankee doodle dandy. Uncle Sam's daughter through and through.

(She smiles.)

I can tell you what's wrong with this country in two simple words. "Lack of glamour". All right, that's three, but "of" shouldn't count. What do you think is wrong with the world? You there, nursing what you hope is top shelf vodka. When you make your way home tonight, just before you lay your head on your pillow, what do you wish for? An end to the internment camps or a pin up cutie like me to help take the edge off? You never thought it could happen again, did you? None of us did. But you're braver than most. You're here, with me, tonight. The sirens outside, the dogs, the thought police, none of them exist. Not tonight. No. Tonight it is just you and me.

(She sits.)

I want to take you back to a time when all women looked like me. It was the least we could do for our boys overseas. There was mom, apple pie and me.

(She lifts her skirt, exposing her legs.)

Nylons, courtesy of the black market. They cost me a day's food rations. Worth every penny, too.

(She picks up a saw and places it vertically between her legs. She smiles at the audience.)

Indulge me if you will.

She picks up a small hammer, hits the saw. A musical sound reverberates.

His name was Johnny.

(She sings Illusions *by Hollander [permission for performance must be obtained from the copyright holder].)*

He was stationed at the front lines. I was the first woman he had seen in months. He came to our first show and asked me, "Doesn't that hurt?" "Nein. I mean, no. Once you know which direction the saw teeth should face it's quite easy. Believe me, you never make that same mistake twice." After that, every show I would look up and there he'd be, always trying to get my attention. Singing along, waving. What a wambunctious wabble wouser my little wedhead was.

(Pauses. Very deliberately pronounces it again.)

What a rambunctious rabble rouser my little redhead was. Just a boy. Far away from home for the first time. Scared, lonely, clinging to me. They all did. I was their fantasy girl come to life. And so, no matter the conditions, the heat, the rain, the bombs bursting in air, I was always in the highest of heels, with a fully made up face and as much décolleté as the generals would allow. You think all this facade is useless until it's used to help people forget where they are. Johnny would always walk me back to my tent after the show and kiss my hand. The perfect gentleman. Filled with dreams and fighting the good fight. I was shipped out while he was gone. No chance for good-byes, just me bouncing in a jeep by moonlight to the next camp. My heart broke a little bit, but I had a job to do, just like him. That night, as I began to play I see a figure way in the back, waving his arms, running to the stage. It was Johnny! My Johnny. "Johnny", I cried out, "are you a wall?" "That's awol, Lili Marlene, and yes I am. But I couldn't let you leave without giving you this." And there, in front of everyone he kissed me. Full on the mouth. A movie kiss, the kind where you lose all sense of place and time and you live in that one little moment locked away forever. The guards took him off stage and he called out to me, "It was worth it, Lili Marlene! No matter what, it was worth it!". I stared after him, alone in a tent full of men calling out my name. I, I picked up my saw and continued. Because that's what a good soldier does. They don't ask questions, they just go on. I never saw him again. But I know that someday my Johnny, he will come back to me. And when he does, I will be weady.

(Stops. Smiles sadly)

Ready.

(She sings the last eight lines of Illusions *again.)*

END OF PLAY

POPS

CHARACTER & SETTING

Thomas

A social worker's office

(The theme to I Love Lucy *plays in the background. The volume comes up then disappears.* TOMAS, *16, stands center stage.)*

TOMAS: Can I just say, I hated Lucy. I used to have to watch it all the time with my Pops. He would call her "La Colora", the Redhead. He thought she was so funny. He'd come home, late at night from work, sneak me out of bed and we'd watch "I Love Lucy" reruns. Now, that was kinda cute when I was a kid, but the older I got the more tired it got, you know what I'm saying? When my father wanted to be funny he'd walk around the house saying *(Thick Desi accent)* "Lucy, splain". My father's English was pretty bad as it is. "Lucy, splain". Funnee Pops. Laugh riot. Parents should never be allowed to try to be funny. So, one night he drags me out of bed again, and I'm so not in the mood, I don't even remember why, and we're sitting there watching Lucy and my father is laughing as loud as Ricky would. You know, almost like he's pronouncing "Ha Ha Ha". And I couldn't take it anymore and I snapped, "Man, why do you think that's still so funny? You've only seen it like a hundred times." My father got real quiet after that and I felt terrible. So I started laughing really hard, trying to make it up to him, you know. But he didn't dare laugh anymore. I think my father thought I was smarter than him so if I told him he shouldn't laugh, then he shouldn't laugh. He went to bed early that night. He was a busboy and he had a breakfast shift the next day at the restaurant where he worked. Windows

on the World at the World Trade Center. He didn't
come home the next day. Or ever. I had to go with my
mother to all these agencies to translate for her, but no
one could help us. "He was a busboy, not a citizen".
I tried to explain it to my mother in Spanish, but she
would just look at them and say, "please, splain". And
people would roll their eyes, or try to be nice or get
impatient and try to get us out of whatever office we
were in. "Busboy, not a citizen." We had the wake in
our apartment, we didn't have a body, of course, just
a picture of my Pops. He was smiling in it. All our
relatives and neighbors were there, and the priest came
by. I stood in a corner, facing away from his picture.
From the laugh I had silenced. I could see my mother
on the sofa, crying quietly, people trying to comfort
her. I turned then, walked up to my father's picture
and outta nowhere, it started, *(In perfect Lucy)* "Are you
tired, run down, listless? Do you poop out at parties?"
The room fell to a dead hush. *(Lucy-like)* "The answer
to all your problems are in this biddle lottle. *(Quickly
corrects himself as Lucy did)* "Little bottle!" My cousins
started to scream with laughter, my uncle looked like
he wanted to kill me and my mother just stared at me.
But I couldn't stop. I was by Lucy possessed. I started
doing all her bits, I was like "Lucy Greatest Hits". Lucy
trapped in the icebox, Lucy as a showgirl with a heavy
headdress, Lucy in the chocolate factory. Pretty soon
everybody is laughing so loud you can barely hear me.
The priest calls out "Do Lucy in the wine vat!". Like
now I'm getting requests?! I look at my mother and she
is laughing so hard tears are flowing down her cheeks.
And when I finally break, when I can't take it anymore,
I cry like Lucy did when Ricky caught her doing
something she shouldn't have. *(Lucy-like)* "Wah!!!!!!!"
(Changing to real pain. Silence) My mother now has
to work two jobs, she wanted us to stay in the U.S.
because that's what my father wanted. The busboy, not

the citizen. He never got a plaque and no one mentions
him or nothing, so I like to think that every time there's
an "I Love Lucy" rerun on that it's a tribute to my
father. And baby, that Colora, she is on twenty four
hours a day.

(Theme to I Love Lucy *returns.)*

END OF PLAY

SILENCE 1

CHARACTERS & SETTING

ROBIN
SANDY

A living room

ROBIN: I'm not speaking to you

(ROBIN *is ignored by* SANDY *who is reading.*)

ROBIN: I mean it.
Fine.

SANDY: Did you say something?

(*Silence*)

(SANDY *goes back to reading.*)

ROBIN: I'm not speaking to you. And it should matter. It should tear you up inside. You should be asking me, no, begging me to talk to you, to tell you what's wrong.

SANDY: I'm sorry, did you say something?

(*Silence*)

ROBIN: How can me not speaking to you not eat you up inside? How can you ignore me? Why do you ignore me? Just look at me, please. Say something. Say something…

SANDY: Something

ROBIN: Aha!

SANDY: Bothering you?

(*Silence*)

ROBIN: These will be the last words I ever say to you. I will never talk to you again. These are the last words. This is the last word. Last. Word.

SANDY: You want to order Chinese?

(ROBIN *just stares at* SANDY.)

ROBIN: …yeah….

END OF PLAY

SILENCE 2

CHARACTERS & SETTING

ROBIN
SANDY

The street

SANDY: I'm not speaking to you.

ROBIN: Oh my God!!!!! NO!!!! Why?!!! What have I done?! Please, please forgive me! I'm so sorry! It was all my fault! I don't deserve you, please, please... *(She throws herself at* SANDY'*s feet and begs.)* You have to forgive me! Please, I'll do anything... I can't live without you, I was wrong, one hundred, one thousand percent wrong....don't leave me, I beg you, I... Oh, God, oh God, I'm gonna die, I'm gonna die....

*(*SANDY *is looking around at the crowd gathering.)*

SANDY: We're kinda in a public place here, Robin.

ROBIN: I don't care, I don't care!!!! You want me to grovel?! I'll do whatever you want, oh God, please talk to me, please don't lock me out, I can't breathe, I'm gonna die... *(She begins to hyperventilate.)*

SANDY: Stop it! Are you crazy?

ROBIN: You want me to be crazy, I'll be crazy! I'll be whatever you want me to be, just please don't stop talking to me!!!

*(*ROBIN, *stops, pulls herself together and gets up and deadeyes* SANDY.*)*

ROBIN: And that, is the proper reaction when the person you supposedly love says they're not gonna talk to you again, asshole!

END OF PLAY

SMILING

CHARACTERS & SETTING

ERNEST
BARTENDER

A bar

(ERNEST, *with a very broad smile plastered on his face, taps on the bar.*)

ERNEST: Am I smiling?

BARTENDER: What?

ERNEST: Am I smiling? Please.

BARTENDER: S'matter, can't you tell? Yeah.

ERNEST: Damn.

(ERNEST *closes his eyes, concentrates very hard, tries to will his smile away.* BARTENDER *watches him.*)

ERNEST: Still?

BARTENDER: Yeah.

ERNEST: Fuck. Fuck-fuck-fuck-fuck-fuck! It's stuck. Every so often my smile gets stuck.

(ERNEST *notices the* BARTENDER *staring at him.*)

ERNEST: Scotch and soda.

(BARTENDER *pours his drink.*)

BARTENDER: Can you drink like that?

ERNEST: No, put a straw in it.

BARTENDER: How exactly does something like that happen?

ERNEST: *(Pointing to his broad smile)* You mean this?

BARTENDER: Kinda.

ERNEST: You ever been in a group? Someone says something, maybe a joke, an astute political comment, some wry reference to something or other, and everybody laughs and nods knowingly. They all get it. I never get it.

(BARTENDER *places a drink with a straw in front of* ERNEST *who takes a sip and then wipes some of the dribble from his smile.*)

ERNEST: Alcohol sometimes helps.

BARTENDER: Understanding stuff or the smile thing?

ERNEST: Nothing helps the smile thing. Just time. I had this same smile plastered on my face for three days once.

BARTENDER: Jesus.

ERNEST: But if I don't smile how will people know I get it. (*He points with his drink to a group seated at a table.*) See them? They are hip personified. They are everything I am not. Cool, savvy, totally ahead of the curve. When they say something, you better get it. Period. They are the tastemakers. The smiling thing started when one of them said something. It was my first time with the group and one of them drops this witty aside and they all look at me. Waiting.

BARTENDER: What did you do?

ERNEST: I nodded. You know, like in recognition. Not enough. So the nod becomes a nervous smile and I'm off the hook. So everytime somebody says something I just smile. I got it down pat. There's the mysterious smile, the fawning smile, and this one, "you're so funny my face hurts" smile. And it does.

BARTENDER: How about if I...

(BARTENDER *is about to put his hands on* ERNEST's *face, but* ERNEST *shakes his head, no.*)

ERNEST: No, when it's stuck, it's stuck. Hey, it's a small price to pay.

BARTENDER: Do they like this smiling person?

ERNEST: Oh yeah.

BARTENDER: Do you?

ERNEST: See that guy, sitting alone in the corner. He's pretending he's really into this song so he won't look so out of place. Every so often he'll look at his watch so that people will think he's waiting for somebody, but he's not. He's downloaded more porn, gone into more chat rooms that any sane human being ever should, but you need some human contact now and then so he's here. And the extent of conversation he'll have this evening is when you ask him, "What'll you have?". You're it for the night, bucko. His problem is he hasn't figured out the smile thing. Gotta get back. I told my little group that their last observation was so brilliant I had to share it with the bartender. *(He pays for his drink.)* By the way, I'm paying for all the drinks at my table. *(He puts down a series of bills, takes his drink.)* Do me a favor. Wave to my little group and smile, so that they can see that just like me, you get it.

(BARTENDER waves and smiles as ERNEST leaves with his drink. After ERNEST leaves, BARTENDER nervously checks to make sure his smile is not frozen.)

END OF PLAY

SPEED DATING FOR THE LATINO ACTOR

CHARACTERS & SETTING

LUIS
YOLI
HECTOR
CARMEN
BENNY

An auditorium

(LUIS stands center, as a WOMAN enters. They shake hands.)

LUIS: Hi, my name is Luis. I'm an actor.

WOMAN: How exciting! Have I seen you in anything?

LUIS: Uh…Cops.

(A bell sounds.)

(DING!)

(The WOMAN now becomes YOLI, another man enters, they shake hands, as LUIS moves on to another woman.)

YOLI: Hi, my name is Yoli, short for Yolanda, I'm an actress.

MAN: Oh, what have I seen you in?

YOLI: I was Pregnant Teen Number Three, in Girl Gangs of Loisaida.

MAN: Direct to video?

YOLI: Shut up.

(DING!)

(ANOTHER WOMAN enters, the MAN now becomes HECTOR. They shake hands as the others continue the ritual silently in the background. Everyone's smiles are becoming more forced.)

LUIS: Hi, my name is Luis.

YOLI: I'm Yoli.

HECTOR: Hi, I'm Hector. I'm an actor.

WOMAN: In what?

HECTOR: In the restaurant I work in, you got a problem with that?!

(DING!)

(The WOMAN *now becomes* CARMEN, *same deal as before.* NEW MAN, *everyone trying to meet and greet in the background. They are all depressed.)*

CARMEN: Hi, I'm Carmen.

LUIS: Luis.

YOLI: Yoli.

HECTOR: Hector.

ALL: I'm an actor.

CARMEN: I'm classically trained. Julliard. Still paying off that loan. I was the hooker who jumped out the window in *Drug Thug II.*

HECTOR: Hey, I was in that!

(DING!)

(The MAN *now becomes* BENNY. *You can cut the depression with a knife.)*

LUIS: Luis.

YOLI: Yeah, whatever Yoli.

HECTOR: Hector.

CARMEN: Carmen.

BENNY: *(He is almost exploding with joy)* Hi, my name is Benny, I'm an actor. I was the corpse in *Law and Order* and they added a flashback so I got a scene with lines and I got to join the union! And I'm an actor! I'm an actor!

*(*BENNY *proudly holds up his Union Card. The others soften and smile at* BENNY, *their hope, however small, returning to them. They all speak proudly.)*

LUIS: I'm an actor.

YOLI: I'm an actor.

HECTOR: I'm an actor.

CARMEN: I'm an actor.

(Everyone on stage)

ALL: And I'm an actor.

END OF PLAY

THE SUBSTITUE

CHARACTER & SETTING

THE SUBSTITUTE

A police interrogation room

(At rise, THE SUBSTITUTE *sits behind a table at a police precint. He is bopping his head to a song only he and the audience can hear, Aretha Franklin's* Respect.*)*

THE SUBSTITUTE: You're right, of course, I shouldn't be smiling. I shouldn't. *(He hides his smile behind his hand.)* You want to know what happened? I'll tell you, and trust me, I won't leave anything out. I'm at school. I'm walking up the stairs, they're narrow. The hand railings are low because they're meant for children, not that any of the students in PS 59 could be classified as children. They are the future young ladies and gentlemen of America. It's the bell between periods, so all of them are running up and down the stairs. I keep to one side, head down, my books close to my side. I'm a substitute teacher. I go where they need me. I hate it. I've been doing it for seven years and I can honestly say I've hated every minute of it. Kids today are not brought up the same way I was. Back then there was respect. At least there was in my family. My parents could take my sister and me anywhere and we knew how to behave. One look from either of them is all it took. Not like today. Punks. Kids are running past me in the stairwell. Some bump into me, but keep going. I always ignore it. But not today. I don't know why. I hold my shoulders out at my side, where they belong, not puffed out, but not like I always do either, like I'm trying to disappear into myself. I feel me bumping into kids for the first time. And it felt good. Let them feel me for a change. I'm entitled to take up space. I have a right to be here. I'm almost at the top of the stairs when

this black girl and I bump shoulders. That's the thing
you see, we bumped into each other. We both did. At
the same time. But she wasn't even looking where she
was going. She was talking to her friends, loud and
cursing. She stops. She's on the step above me, I am
one step away from the landing. And my just having
touched her has enraged her. She screams, no not
screams, that's later, she hollers at me so that everyone
can hear, "Boy, you better watch your fat ass before I
spit in your face!" The stairwell begins to quiet down.
She's found an audience, which I'm sure is all she
wanted, and she really begins to enjoy her anger. I look
up at her. Her face is mocking, seductive. She thinks
she knows me. She's ten minutes into the movie that is
my life, but she knows me. I say quietly, "Excuse me?".
I'm hoping she won't repeat it. That everyone on the
stairwell that witnessed my humiliation will at least
also witness her backing down. "I said, boy you better
watch your fat ass before I spit in your face!". And of
course now there's some laughter, because the first
time some of them missed it. They know they're in for
a show. The sub is actually going to try to reprimand
a student. I very quietly say, "You bumped into me."
There's a part of me that feels trapped, but I also
think she won't do it. One person wouldn't purposely
humiliate another person this way. They wouldn't. I
am smiling now. In a non threatening way. I take a step
up to her so we are both on the landing. And she spits
in my face. The stairwell is rapturous. "Oh, shit! She
did it!" Inside I am dying. Ordinarily I would run away
or wipe the spit off my face and walk past her with,
what I would later try to convince myself was, my
pride intact. Or I would cry and hope I would never
see any of these people again. But not today. I move
closer to her. She spits again in my face. This time it's
more. It lands by her first assault. I don't touch them. I
resist the overwhelming impulse to wipe them off. The

smile on her face is pure pleasure. I'm a forty four year
old man being held hostage by this fourteen, fifteen
year old girl. The students are enjoying this. It's not a
clash of the titans, they already know the outcome, but
they are enjoying every moment of my slow demise.
"Now, why would you want to do that?", I ask. We
are face to face now, and of course she lets loose with
her biggest one yet, have to keep her fans happy. And
I lose myself in her lips, her eyes. I, in that split second,
become obsessed with knocking the smugness off her
face. Replacing it with a look of real surprise, if just for
an instant. I suddenly kiss her. Full force on the mouth.
She pushes me back. Everyone else disappears for
me. I grab her right wrist, because I figure she's right
handed, she'll do me less damage with her left hand,
and I press my entire body into hers, giving her no
space at all to knee me. She's a strong girl. I pull back
and look into her face, she curses at me. I lunge at her
mouth again. The children are shocked into silence.
Some faint calls of "oh shit" seem to be coming from
far away. I pull away, just my head, I look into her face.
I lie and tell her she's so hot. Her breath is ragged now.
She is not fighting me as much, she is almost, dare I say
it, vulnerable. I stick my tongue down her throat, hers
meets mine. And when I finally feel her silky tongue
in my mouth I bite down with all the force I have. All
the years of resentment and pushed back anger. She
screams and I push her into the kids down the stairs.
She doesn't travel much, they were almost on top of us
watching my presumed castration. They see the blood
oozing from her mouth and hear her screaming. And
I spit the piece of her tongue at her. That piece of meat
that once belonged to her. "That", I tell her, "is how
you spit into somebody's face". It's pandemonium as I
turn and continue up to my classroom. Her blood and
spit still on my face and in my mouth. I sat at my desk
waiting for students that never came, until you arrived,

my stomach doing somersaults, my heart racing. Yes,
I did a terrible thing. But I at least did something. And
she and every kid in that stairwell will think twice
about picking on somebody just because they think
they're an easy mark. You walk around with a gun all
day, officer, what would you know about slow and
constant humiliation? I did it. Me. I changed the look
on her face. Forever. So yes, whatever you need me
to sign, I'll sign it. Just make sure you spell my name
right. Give credit where credit is due.

END OF PLAY